J
993
New

SEP 1997

New Zealand in pic-
tures

DUE DATE

11/97	1X		
11/04 7X			

Visual Geography Series®

NEW ZEALAND

...in Pictures

Prepared by
Geography Department

Lerner Publications Company
Minneapolis

Courtesy of New Zealand Tourist and Publicity Office

**The Beehive, completed in 1981, houses parliamentary of-
fices in Wellington, New Zealand's capital.**

This book is an all-new edition in the Visual Geography Series. Previous editions were published by
Sterling Publishing Company, New York City. The
text, set in 10/12 Century Textbook, is fully revised
and updated, and new photographs, maps, charts, and
captions have been added.

LIBRARY OF CONGRESS CATALOGING-IN-PUBLICATION DATA

New Zealand in Pictures / prepared by Geography Department, Lerner Publications Company
    p. cm. — (Visual geography series)
    Rev. ed. of: New Zealand in pictures / prepared by
Michael Robson.
    Includes index.
    Summary: Text and photographs introduce the
topography, history, society, economy, and governmental structure of New Zealand.
    ISBN 0-8225-1862-7
    1. New Zealand. [1. New Zealand] I. Robson, Michael,
fl. 1964– New Zealand in pictures. II. Lerner Publications Company. Geography Dept. III. Series: Visual geography series (Minneapolis, Minn.)
DU408.N48   1990
993—dc20   89–36541
                                        CIP
                                        AC

International Standard Book Number: 0-8225-1862-7
Library of Congress Catalog Card Number: 89-36541

VISUAL GEOGRAPHY SERIES®

Publisher
Harry Jonas Lerner
Associate Publisher
Nancy M. Campbell
Senior Editor
Mary M. Rodgers
Editors
Gretchen Bratvold
Dan Filbin
Phyllis Schuster
Photo Researchers
Karen A. Sirvaitis
Kerstin Coyle
Editorial/Photo Assistant
Marybeth Campbell
Consultants/Contributors
Ward Barrett
Sandra K. Davis
Designer
Jim Simondet
Cartographer
Carol F. Barrett
Indexers
Kristine S. Schubert
Sylvia Timian
Production Manager
Gary J. Hansen

Courtesy of Ward Barrett

**Underground thermal activity creates a steam vent near a
home in Rotorua on the North Island's Volcanic Plateau.**

Acknowledgments

Title page photo by Ward Barrett.

Elevation contours adapted from *The Times Atlas of
the World,* seventh comprehensive edition (New York:
Times Books, 1985).

2 3 4 5 6 JR 99 98 97 96 95

A Maori woman swings balls made of fiber while performing the traditional *poi* (ball) dance. In time to the soft rhythm of singers, the dancer sways and continuously twirls the poi over her shoulders and to her sides, thighs, knees, and head. The Maori were New Zealand's first inhabitants.

Courtesy of New Zealand Tourist and Publicity Office

Contents

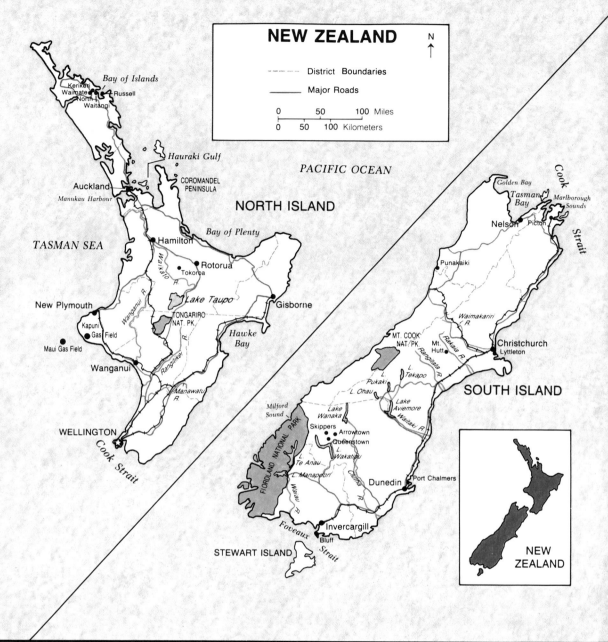

NEW ZEALAND

N ↑

- – – – District Boundaries
- ——— Major Roads

| 0 | 50 | 100 Miles |
| 0 | 50 | 100 Kilometers |

Bay of Islands
Kerikeri
Waimate
North
Waitangi
Russell

Hauraki Gulf

PACIFIC OCEAN

Auckland
Manukau Harbour

COROMANDEL
PENINSULA

NORTH ISLAND

TASMAN SEA

Hamilton
Bay of Plenty

Waikato R.

Rotorua
Tokoroa

Wanganui R.

Lake Taupo

Gisborne

New Plymouth
Kapuni
Gas Field
Maui Gas Field

TONGARIRO
NAT. PK.

Rangitikei R.

Hawke Bay

Wanganui

Manawatu R.

WELLINGTON

Cook Strait

Golden Bay
Tasman Bay
Marlborough Sounds

Cook Strait

Nelson
Picton

Punakaiki

Waimakariri R.

MT. COOK
NAT. PK.
Mt. Hutt
Rakaia R.

Christchurch
Lyttleton

SOUTH ISLAND

L. Pukaki
L. Ohau
L. Tekapo

Lake
Aviemore
Waitaki R.

Milford
Sound

Lake
Wanaka

Skippers
Arrowtown
Queenstown

L. Te Anau

L. Wakatipu

FIORDLAND NATIONAL PARK

L. Manapouri

Waiau R.

Clutha R.

Dunedin
Port Chalmers

Invercargill
Bluff

Foveaux Strait

STEWART ISLAND

NEW ZEALAND

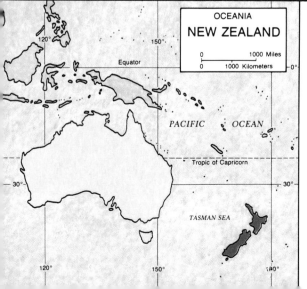

OCEANIA
NEW ZEALAND

| 0 | 1000 Miles |
| 0 | 1000 Kilometers |

120°
150°
Equator
0°
PACIFIC OCEAN
Tropic of Capricorn
30°
30°
TASMAN SEA
120°
150°
180°

METRIC CONVERSION CHART
To Find Approximate Equivalents

WHEN YOU KNOW:	MULTIPLY BY:	TO FIND:
AREA		
acres	0.41	hectares
square miles	2.59	square kilometers
CAPACITY		
gallons	3.79	liters
LENGTH		
feet	30.48	centimeters
yards	0.91	meters
miles	1.61	kilometers
MASS (weight)		
pounds	0.45	kilograms
tons	0.91	metric tons
VOLUME		
cubic yards	0.77	cubic meters
TEMPERATURE		
degrees Fahrenheit	0.56 (*after* subtracting 32)	degrees Celsius

Small emerald-colored lakes fill pockets in the volcanic soil of Mount Ngauruhoe on the North Island. Ngauruhoe, an active volcano that formed within the last 2,500 years, erupted with lava flows in 1870, 1949, and 1954. Gases laden with ash spewed from its cone in 1974 and 1975.

Introduction

An island nation in the South Pacific Ocean, New Zealand is small in both population and area. Its islands reached their present size and shape only about five million years ago—a short time on a geologic scale. Forces that caused the earth's crust to buckle and form New Zealand continue to push the tallest mountain ranges upward. Volcanic activity and earthquakes are also still changing the physical features of the country.

New Zealand's history as an inhabited land is of recent origin as well. The country's first people, the Maori, arrived from an island in Polynesia, far to the north, about 1,200 years ago. The Maori created a culture that was unaffected by outside contacts until the late 1700s, when European explorers reached the islands. British settlers began moving to New Zealand in the early 1800s and became the majority population by 1860.

The Maori and Europeans adjusted peacefully in most regions, but in areas where many Maori lived, disputes over land led to warfare. After the Land Wars ended in 1872, the country turned its attention to the expansion of farming and to the development of roads, railways, and manufacturing.

Although it was under Britain's authority until 1947, New Zealand has been largely self-governing since the mid-1800s. Living far from the world's major continents, New Zealanders proved to be self-reliant people who devised their own practical solutions to problems that arose.

The most serious challenges facing New Zealand in modern times have been economic ones. For much of its income, New Zealand sells agricultural products to other nations. When foreign demand for those products falls, the country's economy declines. In the early 1970s, Britain—New Zealand's largest trading partner—decided to buy more products from Europe and fewer from New Zealand. Faced with an economic crisis, the government turned to social welfare programs to maintain the nation's standard of living. Such programs had helped the country before, but this time they did not work.

After several years with a weak economy and high unemployment, New Zealanders decided to make their government smaller and to sell goods to more countries. These changes took years to accomplish and made life harder for the many New Zealanders who depended on government support, but economic conditions started to improve in the mid-1990s. Keeping the economy strong will be the country's top priority in the coming years.

Merino sheep, brought in from higher pastures, wait in pens for eye clippings and checkups at Glentanner Station in the Canterbury region of the South Island. The station (ranch) lies at the base of the Ben Ohau Range.

The Pancake Rocks—eroded limestone formations that resemble stacks of giant pancakes—trap surf in narrow passages called blowholes. Incoming waves force the water up and back to the ocean in explosive bursts. The unusual rocks are situated on the South Island's western coast near Punakaiki.

Courtesy of Richard Southward

1) The Land

Located midway between the equator and the South Pole, New Zealand lies 1,200 miles southeast of Australia. The Tasman Sea, which is part of the Pacific Ocean, separates the two nations. Covering an area of 103,736 square miles, New Zealand is about the size of the state of Colorado. Two main islands—the North Island and the South Island—form most of the country's territory. Stewart Island—which lies off the southern tip of the South Island— and many smaller pieces of territory are also part of New Zealand.

Three-fourths of New Zealand's 3.5 million people live on the North Island—an area of 44,244 square miles. Cook Strait separates this landmass from the South Island, which covers 58,965 square miles.

Courtesy of Richard Southward

Queenstown, a center for gold miners in the 1860s, sits on the shores of Lake Wakatipu. Now a popular resort, this small city of 3,600 attracts skiers in winter and seekers of mountain scenery year-round.

Each of the two islands is narrow and about 500 miles long. No part of the country is more than 80 miles from the sea. Including the distances added by bays and fiords (long inlets of sea), New Zealand's coastline measures 4,300 miles.

Topography

Most of New Zealand is mountainous or hilly. A high range—the Southern Alps—extends almost the entire length of the South Island. The alps contain 17 peaks that rise above 10,000 feet. The mountains of the North Island are lower but very rugged, and they divide into many ranges. Volcanic eruptions created that island's tallest peaks.

THE NORTH ISLAND

The high Volcanic Plateau occupies the center of the North Island. This region contains three active volcanoes—Mount Ruapehu (9,175 feet), Mount Ngauruhoe (7,515 feet), and Mount Tongariro (6,458 feet). At the northern end of the plateau, hot rocks in the earth's crust heat underground water to produce unusual thermal features. These include geysers, steam vents, hot springs, boiling mud, and simmering lakes.

Steep hills lie south and east of the Volcanic Plateau. The southernmost ranges—which extend to Cook Strait—form the Wairarapa region, where many earthquakes occur. West of the plateau, mountainous country merges into Taranaki, a dairy-farming area on the lower slopes of a big, dormant volcano—Mount Taranaki.

To the north, low hills and fertile river valleys form the Waikato region, which contains New Zealand's most productive farmland. Beyond Waikato are two peninsulas—Northland and Coromandel. Auckland, New Zealand's largest city, sits at the base of Northland, a 220-mile-long arm of land with high hills and many harbors. Farther east lies the shorter Coromandel Peninsula, which is mountainous and mostly undeveloped.

THE SOUTH ISLAND

Dominating the South Island, the Southern Alps extend from the Marlborough Sounds of the northern coast to Fiordland in the southwestern corner. Mount Cook, New Zealand's highest peak at 12,349 feet, rises from the center of the alps. The Maori call the mountain *Aorangi,* which means "the cloud piercer."

Thousands of years ago, glaciers formed in the Southern Alps, and many of these slow-moving bodies of ice remain. The 18-mile-long Tasman Glacier on the eastern side of Mount Cook is one of the world's largest ice masses not in the polar regions.

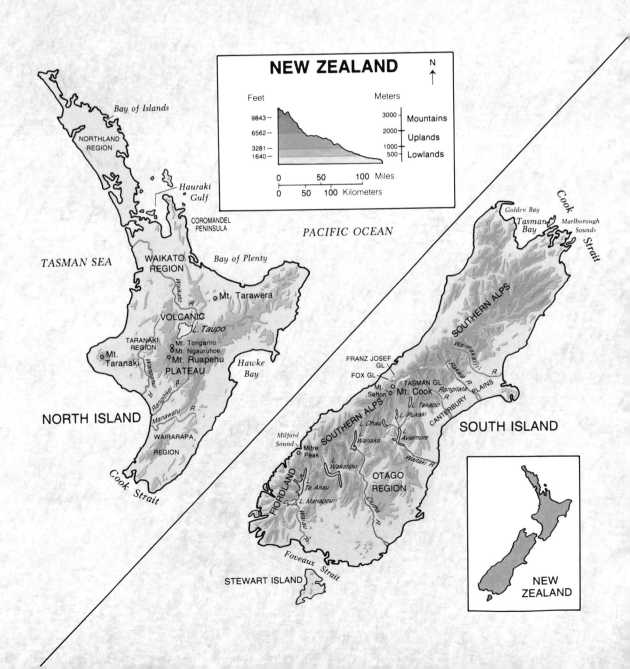

Courtesy of Gladys Green

A geyser erupts in Rotorua, one of the world's few areas with many types of geothermal activity. Underground pockets of steam in the region also produce bubbling mud, simmering lakes, and steam vents.

The Fox and the Franz Josef glaciers stretch 8 miles and 6 miles, respectively, down the western slopes of the alps to the edge of a coastal rain-forest.

New Zealand's most extensive lowland—the Canterbury Plains—lies east of the Southern Alps. The Rangitata, Rakaia, and other rivers helped to create these flatlands by depositing rocks, gravel, sand, and soil from the mountains. The plains, which are about 100 miles long and 40 miles wide, attracted early European settlers because the land was easy to farm. The region is now the country's major grain-growing area.

The southeastern portion of the South Island—the Otago plateaus and basins—is the driest and, in summer, the hottest part of New Zealand. Much of Otago consists of craggy hills and deep ravines. In the 1860s, gold discoveries in Otago drew many immigrants to New Zealand.

Courtesy of New Zealand Tourist and Publicity Office

The highest peak in the Southern Alps, Mount Cook (12,349 feet) is distinguished by its triangular form as well as by its massive size. The mountain's summit ridge is one mile long.

The Waimakariri River, at this point leaving the Southern Alps, is one of many broad waterways that cross the Canterbury Plains. The rivers built the plains by carrying gravel, silt, and debris from the mountains. The Waimakariri reaches the Pacific Ocean north of the city of Christchurch.

After the gold ran out, sheep raising provided the main income for the region. In recent years, hydroelectric and irrigation projects on the Clutha River have broadened Otago's agricultural output.

Rivers and Lakes

New Zealand's many swift rivers are difficult to navigate but valuable as sources of hydroelectric power. On the North Island, the 264-mile Waikato River rises near Mount Ruapehu, enters Lake Taupo, and flows out of the lake in a winding course to the Tasman Sea. The government has built dams on the Waikato to produce hydroelectric power. Three major waterways—the Wanganui, the Rangitikei, and the Manawatu—run southwest from the Volcanic Plateau to the Tasman Sea.

Many rivers begin in the lakes of the Southern Alps. Two of the waterways—the Clutha and Waitaki—are major sources of hydropower. The Clutha, New Zealand's largest river in volume, starts in Lake Wanaka and travels through the Otago region on its 200-mile journey to the Pacific Ocean. The broad Waitaki River forms the boundary between Otago and the Canterbury Plains. The 130-mile waterway is fed by rivers from Lakes Tekapo, Pukaki, and Ohau.

Lake Taupo, New Zealand's largest body of water, covers 234 square miles in the center of the North Island's Volcanic Plateau. A violent eruption that occurred about A.D. 135 opened the massive crater that forms the lake bed. The volcano's rocks and debris built the plateau that surrounds Lake Taupo.

11

Courtesy of New Zealand Tourist and Publicity Office

A rain-forest surrounds trampers (hikers) on Milford Track, a 34-mile-long trail that runs from Lake Te Anau to Milford Sound. The route leads through open mountain country as well as forests, and it passes Sutherland Falls, the world's fifth highest waterfall.

On the South Island, ancient glaciers carved many deep valleys, now filled with lakes, in the alps. The largest in area is Lake Te Anau, whose narrow arms reach into the mountains. The Upper Waiau River connects Lake Te Anau to Lake Manapouri—New Zealand's biggest lake by volume of water and an important source of hydroelectricity. Northwest of Lake Te Anau is the country's longest body of water, 52-mile-long Lake Wakatipu.

Climate

On New Zealand's coasts, where most of the population live, the climate is mild year-round. At sea level, the country's average temperature drops about 10 degrees from north to south. Subtropical weather occurs on the northern peninsulas, and subarctic temperatures are recorded in the high elevations of the alps. Some regions, especial-

ly on the southern coasts of each island, are very windy.

Since New Zealand is in the Southern Hemisphere, midwinter comes in July, and midsummer occurs in January. In Auckland, on the North Island, the average daytime temperature in January reaches 79° and the nighttime low is 53° F. In July corresponding readings are 62° and 38° F. Greater ranges in daily temperature occur on the South Island. In the city of Christchurch, for example, the low on a January day is typically 41° and the high reaches 86° F. Average lows and highs in July are 26° and 61° F.

Rain falls fairly evenly throughout the year in New Zealand. On the South Island, however, the high mountains make a barrier that affects the way rainfall is distributed to various regions. Most air masses move in from the west. Blocked by the alps, the air rises, dropping its moisture on the coast and western slopes. Thus, the coastal rain-forest at the western base of the alps receives more than 200 inches of rain annually. Because the air loses moisture as it crosses the mountains, some parts of Otago on the eastern side get only 13 inches of precipitation each year.

Flora and Fauna

More than 2,000 varieties of ferns, evergreens, and flowering plants are native to New Zealand. Before humans arrived, 80 percent of the islands were densely forested. The Maori burned about one-third of the trees to clear land for crops, to obtain timber, and to force hunted animals into the open. European settlers removed an additional one-third of the forests.

The widespread destruction of trees in the last century caused serious erosion problems in some parts of New Zealand. The practice also destroyed the habitats of some animals that existed nowhere else in the world. Among present-day New Zealanders, concern about the environment is

Lupines add color to mountain meadows during summer in New Zealand. Species of lupine appear throughout the world, but many forms of vegetation that are native to New Zealand grow nowhere else.

Courtesy of Richard Southward

13

The Maori call this 1,200-year-old tree *Tane Mahuta*—which means "King of the Kauri." It grows in the Waipoua Kauri Forest of the Northland peninsula. Kauri forests became important to the development of New Zealand soon after the Maori arrived from Polynesia. The trees have furnished wood for canoes, ship masts, and buildings. In the late 1800s, European immigrants dug in forest soils for deposits of kauri gum—the sap from ancient trees—to use in making high-quality varnishes and resins. Alarmed that kauri forests were being wiped out, conservationists in the 1940s persuaded the government to protect remaining stands of the tree.

very high. Conservationists, often working cooperatively with government departments, have achieved considerable success in protecting the country's unusual plants and animals.

New Zealand's native evergreens include the rimu, totara, kahikatea, and kauri. The giant kauri can live for 2,000 years, reaching 200 feet in height. Great stands of the tree once grew on the northern peninsulas. In the 1800s, however, shipbuilders prized this timber so highly that loggers nearly destroyed the kauri forests. Laws protect remaining stands of the tree. Native beech forests still occupy regions in the western alps on the South Island.

Broad-leaved trees—such as the karaka and red-blossomed pohutukawa—grow in coastal forests. Many varieties of ferns—some 50 feet tall—cover forest floors. The silver fern is the country's official emblem. In the mountains, vegetation has adapted to cold, windy conditions. Plant species that thrive in high elevations include daisies, nicotiania (a flowering shrub) and cushion plants. An unusual coastal plant is the cabbage tree—a giant lily with spear-shaped foliage.

Only one mammal, the bat, is native to New Zealand, but many flightless birds and insects evolved there. Perhaps the most remarkable bird to live on the islands was the giant moa. By the seventeenth century, however, the Maori had hunted this 10-foot-tall plant-eater to extinction. A small relative of the moa—the kiwi—has

Found only on certain small coastal islands of New Zealand, the tuatara is the sole survivor of a family of reptiles that existed more than 100 million years ago. The tuatara, which resembles an iguana, can live for as long as 300 years and can grow to two-and-one-half feet in length.

become a national symbol. In fact, New Zealanders call themselves Kiwis after the shy brown bird of their forests.

Among New Zealand's other flightless birds are the kakapo (a large parrot that lives under tree roots), the weka (wood hen), the pukeko (swamp hen), and the takahe. Thought for many years to be extinct, the takahe is a large bird with blue and green feathers, a red bill, and red legs. Many species of birds that fly died out after humans began cutting New Zealand's forests. Among those that survived are two frequently heard songbirds, the tui and the bellbird.

The kea, or mountain parrot, inhabits the open country of the South Island. The birds engage in playful antics, such as sliding down rooftops. For many years, farmers blamed keas for killing sheep. Although the birds do scavenge on dead sheep, they do not kill the live animals.

The kiwi, a flightless bird that is active at night, has become a national symbol of New Zealand. The male kiwi builds the nest and, always facing south, sits for 80 days on the large egg that the female lays. The bird's feathers resemble hair. Its long bill, which has nostrils at the tip, is useful for digging worms. At one time, the Maori decorated their cloaks with kiwi feathers. European immigrants used the bird's hollow legs for pipestems and cooked the meat into kiwi pie. Kiwis are now protected by law.

Courtesy of New Zealand Tourist and Publicity Office

Photo by Geoff Moon

The colorful, rare takahe, a marsh hen, is a flightless bird that was thought to have become extinct in the last century. In 1948, however, several hundred pairs of the birds were discovered near Lake Te Anau. They are now protected in a preserve, and their numbers are increasing.

A horse-drawn carriage offers visitors a leisurely ride through downtown Christchurch, which was founded in 1850 on marshy flat land in the Canterbury Plains. The city's famous Anglican (Church of England) cathedral is in the background. Its English settlers wanted Christchurch to resemble their homeland.

Cities

With 85 percent of its people living in cities, New Zealand is one of the most urbanized of modern countries. Auckland is the largest urban area in the country. Ranking next in size are Wellington, Christchurch, Hamilton, and Dunedin.

Auckland, with a population of about 886,000, is New Zealand's leading financial and industrial center. Nearly surrounded by water, the city occupies a narrow neck of land west of the Hauraki Gulf. Waitemata Harbour, which is deep and easy to navigate, forms Auckland's northern boundary and goes into the gulf. Manukau Harbour, which lies to the south and west, is muddy and shallow but can accommodate small ships.

Long before European colonists arrived, Maori groups discovered the fertile soil of the Auckland area. They built fortresses on the sides and in the craters of extinct volcanoes in the region. After Europeans settled there, the availability of flatland and a fine harbor drew industry to the site. In recent decades, job opportunities in Auckland have attracted thousands of Pacific Islanders as well as people from other parts of New Zealand.

Wellington, New Zealand's capital, lies on the southern tip of the North Island on a deep, circular harbor. Steep hills surround the city. The hills are bounded by active fault lines that have the potential to cause destructive earthquakes. Many of Wellington's 326,000 residents work for the national government, but a variety of businesses also operate in the capital.

Located 65 miles south of Auckland, Hamilton is the largest inland city in New Zealand. With a population of 149,000, Hamilton serves as a hub for the Waikato region's dairy and beef farms. The city contains several agricultural research facilities and many industries.

Christchurch (population 307,000) is the biggest urban center on the South Island. The Canterbury Association in Britain—which included officials of the Church of England and some members of the British Parliament—helped to found the city in 1850. One of the group's goals was to build a city with a distinctly English appearance. Lying near the eastern coast almost halfway down the South Island, Christchurch is the industrial center of the Canterbury Plains. With fine port facilities at nearby Lyttleton and an international airport, the city also serves as a base for Antarctic research.

Two hundred miles south of Christchurch is Dunedin (population 110,000), which Scottish immigrants settled in 1848. In the 1860s, prospectors flocked to Dunedin when gold was discovered in the Otago region. The city flourished as New Zealand's financial hub until gold supplies ran out toward the end of the decade. Its citizens then turned to farming and industry. Dunedin is the home of the University of Otago, the oldest of New Zealand's seven universities.

Courtesy of New Zealand Tourist and Publicity Office

The commercial center of Auckland adjoins Waitemata Harbour. The residential areas and suburbs of New Zealand's largest city sprawl beyond nearby hills, interrupted in places by dormant volcanic cones on which the Maori once built their homes.

The Scottish settlers who founded Dunedin regarded education as a priority, and they quickly established New Zealand's first university—the University of Otago. This building, one of the oldest at the school, was built in 1878. Many modern structures have been added to the campus in recent years.

Photo by Ted Scott

Courtesy of New Zealand Tourist and Publicity Office

Hills rise steeply behind the downtown buildings of Wellington, New Zealand's capital. The city surrounds a fine harbor on Cook Strait at the southern end of the North Island. Because of the strong gusts that blow across the strait, Wellington is called the windy city.

To protect their crops and people from enemies, Maori groups built fortified villages—called *pa*—in locations that were easy to defend. Wooden stockades protect this pa, which was constructed on an island.

2) History and Government

Archaeological findings indicate that the first inhabitants of New Zealand were the Maori, who migrated from eastern Polynesia sometime between A.D. 700 and 1000. Their ancestral island, which they called *Hawaiki,* was probably near Tahiti. Historians do not know whether the Maori found New Zealand by accident—by being blown off course while seeking another destination—or by plan. Nor have researchers determined whether the Maori came in one large migration or in numerous voyages that lasted into the fourteenth century.

The Maori had no written language, but they did have a rich storytelling tradition. According to their legends, a Polynesian fisherman named Kupe discovered the islands around A.D. 925. He called them *Aotearoa,* meaning "the land of the long white cloud." Kupe explored Aotearoa,

This quiet spot on Golden Bay lies near the site where a Dutch expedition led by Abel Tasman attempted to land in 1642. Attacked by the Maori, Tasman's boats never reached shore.

but, finding the region uninhabited and disliking the cool climate, he returned to Hawaiki. Generations of Maori heard Kupe's stories of Aotearoa. Eventually, some of his people set out in large oceangoing canoes to settle the faraway islands.

The Moa Hunters

Although scholars respect the Maori legends, they rely on site excavations, language studies, and comparisons with other Polynesian peoples to learn about the settlement of New Zealand. Archaeologists have determined that in order to survive most of the earliest Maori in New Zealand fished and hunted moa and other birds. These Maori—called Moa Hunters—followed a simple way of life.

Most of the early Maori lived on the South Island, where the largest species of moa were plentiful. By A.D.1100 the Moa Hunter culture was well-established. In

Maori carvers lavished great skill on war canoes. Using stone axes and shell-tipped drills, they built the canoes—which could be 80 feet long—from kauri trees. Such canoes were among the people's most precious possessions.

Drawing by Murray Webb, Courtesy of Cambridge University Press

Early generations of Maori in New Zealand relied on the giant moa, a flightless bird, as their main source of meat. Many giant moa once roamed the plains of the South Island. By 1500, however, the birds were becoming rare, and by 1700 Maori groups had hunted the giant moa to extinction.

the northern parts of the North Island, however, Maori groups had begun to develop a society based on agriculture. They grew starchy root crops from Polynesia—*kumaras* (sweet potatoes), taros, and yams —and cultivated native ferns, whose roots were nourishing.

In the 1300s, food supplies in Aotearoa began to dwindle. The number of moa decreased, and Moa Hunters burned wooded areas to dislodge the birds. As forests disappeared, rain washed soil from hills into rivers, ruining fishing areas. In addition, the weather grew cold and stormy when a period called the Little Ice Age arrived during the 1500s. Farmed plots lost their fertility, and storms made it hard to

clear additional land. As conditions worsened, the Moa Hunter culture declined.

Classic Maori Culture

In the north, however, the Maori who relied on agriculture were able to meet the challenge of a colder, stormier climate. They learned to use storage pits to preserve food supplies during the winter, and they designed buildings and clothing to protect themselves from the weather. These groups developed a way of life that archaeologists now call the Classic Maori culture.

By the eighteenth century, the Maori on the North Island were skilled farmers, builders, and weavers. Using stone tools, they also excelled at wood carving. The Maori developed a religion that regarded many places, people, events, and features of the land and sea as sacred. Each Maori group's prestige was linked to its land, which warriors were willing to protect with their lives.

About 50 *iwi* (Maori groups) established themselves in New Zealand. Within each iwi, closely related families formed *hapu*—or clans—and held land in common. In most hapu, members lived in houses within or close to a *pa*—an area protected by natural boundaries, wooden stockades,

and terraces. Families retreated to the pa during warfare. By fighting, warriors hoped to revenge wrongs committed against their people. Victors in battle insulted their enemies by eating those they had slain. Captives from defeated hapu became slaves in other hapu.

European Exploration

The Maori's first contact with non-Polynesian peoples probably occurred in 1642 when the Dutch navigator Abel Tasman reached Golden Bay on the northwestern

This Maori warrior, drawn by an artist who accompanied Captain James Cook to New Zealand, wears a feathered cloak that indicates his high rank. When Europeans arrived in the late 1700s, Maori men wore their hair in a knot on top of the head, along with a decorative comb and two or more feathers.

corner of the South Island. The Maori used canoes to attack one of the expedition's landing boats, and lives were lost on both sides. Tasman sailed away without setting foot on the islands, which the Dutch government later named Nieuw Zeeland. More than 125 years passed before the Maori again saw Europeans.

In 1769 the British navy sent Captain James Cook in the ship *Endeavour* to explore the South Pacific. Cook arrived in New Zealand in October 1769 and encountered Maori at many of his landing sites. Unlike Tasman's experience with the Maori, these meetings were usually friendly. Cook came to admire the people's resourcefulness.

A Polynesian who had joined the *Endeavour* in Tahiti was able to interpret the Maori language, enabling the crew to trade goods with the people. The expedition's scientists collected samples of plant life. Cook spent 176 days charting New Zealand and produced a very accurate map of the main islands. The captain and others in his party published accounts of New Zealand after this journey and after two later voyages to the South Pacific.

Pakehas Arrive

For 20 years after Cook's voyages, few *pakehas* (the Maori word for persons of European descent) landed in New Zealand. But a growing demand in Europe for sealskins and whale oil in the 1790s sent seal-hunting and whaling ships to New Zealand's coastal waters. Sailors anchored their vessels in the Bay of Islands on the eastern coast of the Northland Peninsula, and villages sprang up along its harbors in the early 1800s.

Courtesy of James Ford Bell Library, University of Minnesota

Captain James Cook, exploring the South Pacific for the British government, landed near present-day Gisborne, New Zealand, in October 1769. Sailing the coasts, Cook spent six months mapping the country. By treating the Maori well wherever his expedition anchored, Cook gained the people's trust and assistance.

Settlers in Kororareka built Christ Church, the oldest church in New Zealand, in 1836. The town, which was later called Russell, was one of the earliest points of contact between the Maori and Europeans. Buried in the churchyard are sailors from HMS *Hazard* who died in 1845 while defending Kororareka during a Maori rebellion.

The region's kauri trees provided long, sturdy timbers for ship masts, and native flax plants yielded fiber for rope. Traders in New South Wales, Australia—a British colony—began sailing to New Zealand. Soon ships from the United States and European countries were also arriving in the Bay of Islands. Trade created jobs for many Maori. They cut timber, prepared flax, and served on ships' crews.

Although Cook had explored New Zealand for Britain, that nation showed little interest at first in colonizing the area. With no authorities to make or enforce regulations, Kororareka (present-day Russell) and other coastal villages on the Bay of Islands earned a reputation for lawlessness. Among the inhabitants of these outposts were escaped convicts from Australia and runaway sailors.

A different type of pakeha soon arrived in New Zealand, however. Samuel Marsden, a Church of England missionary in Australia, established the first Christian mission in the Bay of Islands area in 1814. He recruited a staff in Britain to teach the Maori practical skills and convert them to Christianity. When Henry Williams arrived to direct the mission in 1823, he translated the Bible into Maori and taught reading and writing. Using the Bible to learn to read, the Maori also absorbed Christian teachings, and by 1830 a few had converted to Christianity. As missionary work spread, the Maori way of life began to change.

25

This painting of Tamati Waka Nene by New Zealand artist Gottfried Lindauer shows the facial markings that were typical of great Maori leaders. Tattooing, which involved carving the skin with a stone adz (cutting tool), was a painful process that took several months. More tattoos were added as a person's importance increased.

Edward Gibbon Wakefield organized the New Zealand Company in London in 1837.

The other pakehas with whom the Maori dealt—traders, sailors, and adventurers—affected Maori society more quickly. Those Europeans introduced guns, new diseases, and liquor into New Zealand. Guns made some Maori leaders—including Hongi Hika, a chief in the Bay of Islands—very powerful. With a force of 2,000 warriors, Hongi Hika attacked other North Island Maori in the early 1820s to settle disputes.

Infectious diseases posed another threat to the Maori, who had lived for centuries in isolation and had no natural protection against European illnesses. As guns, sickness, and alcohol spread among the Maori, their population—which probably numbered about 250,000 when Cook came to New Zealand—declined rapidly.

British Colonization

Fewer than 2,000 Europeans lived in New Zealand in the late 1830s, but speculators scrambled to obtain Maori land. Among the eager buyers were representatives of the New Zealand Company, which Edward Gibbon Wakefield had founded in Britain. Wakefield, who wanted to promote the orderly settlement of New Zealand, raised money by selling shares in the company to wealthy investors. With those funds, the company purchased land and arranged for the transportation of British tradespeople and laborers. Wakefield intended that these groups would be the workers in the company's settlements.

As pressure to make New Zealand a colony increased, the British government in 1839 sent Captain William Hobson to administer the islands and safeguard Maori interests. At Waitangi in 1840, Hobson offered Maori leaders a proposal to bring New Zealand into the British Empire. In return for granting Britain authority over the islands, the Maori would receive clear possession of their remaining lands and full status as British citizens. In addition, the Maori would sell land only to the British government.

On February 6, 1840, Maori leaders signed the Treaty of Waitangi, which made New Zealand a colony of Great Britain. The date is now celebrated as New Zealand's national day.

Hobson and other British officials believed the document would protect the Maori from being cheated in land deals. After a day of discussion, most Maori leaders who were present decided to accept the terms, and they signed the Treaty of Waitangi on February 6, 1840.

The agreement made New Zealand a British colony. Hobson moved the capital from Kororareka to the south side of Waitemata Harbour. The new capital, Auckland, soon became a trading center. The New Zealand Company established settlements in Wellington and Wanganui in 1840 and in New Plymouth and Nelson in 1842. With the aid of the Free Church of Scotland, the company also founded Dunedin in 1848. With the Canterbury Association in England, it established Christchurch in 1850.

Farms and towns developed more rapidly on the South Island, where the Canterbury Plains provided treeless, fertile land for raising sheep and crops. Two obstacles

Captain William Hobson, who became the first governor of New Zealand, drew up the Treaty of Waitangi. Hobson hoped the agreement would protect the Maori from dishonest land buyers as the British began to settle New Zealand. By the time of Hobson's death in 1842, however, disputes between the Maori and settlers over land claims were common.

discouraged early immigrants from making their homes on the North Island. One was the thick forest that had to be cleared for farming. The second was the presence of strong Maori clans that showed growing resistance to parting with their land.

A few years after signing the Treaty of Waitangi, some Maori leaders began to reconsider the agreement. They realized that they could no longer sell land to private individuals but only to the government. They also saw Europeans reselling property for many times the original price.

In addition, as Auckland expanded, it replaced the Bay of Islands as a center of trade, which hurt the Maori economy. In the mid-1840s the powerful Maori leader Hone Heke led uprisings in the area north of Auckland to protest unfair treatment by the pakehas. After a year of fighting, the colonial troops of Governor George Grey—who replaced Hobson in 1845—defeated the rebels.

In 1852 Grey drafted laws that made New Zealand largely self-governing. The national Parliament, which first met in 1854, consisted of the Legislative Council, whose members were appointed by the governor-general, and the elected House of Representatives. Only male European landowners could vote for representatives.

The Stone Store at Kerikeri in the Bay of Islands was built to hold mission supplies. The building housed British ammunition in the 1840s, when the Maori leader Hone Heke led rebellions against colonial authorities.

The dormant volcano Mount Taranaki (also called Mount Egmont) was a sacred place to the Maori. Believing that European settlers had moved onto their land illegally, the Taranaki Maori responded with raids and warfare during the Land Wars of the 1860s. In the 1870s, a group of Maori formed a commune near Mount Taranaki's western slopes. Led by Te Whiti, they protested the Birtish presence until colonial troops destroyed the village in 1881.

Courtesy of Richard Southward

The Land Wars

In 1855 the Maori were still the largest population in the colony. They grew most of the food supply and controlled coastal shipping. Many Maori shared in the development of New Zealand by working to build roads and houses. Because of mission schools and government programs, some Maori could read and write.

Within several years, however, the pakehas outnumbered the Maori. The continuing stream of immigrants alarmed many Maori. Some Maori groups on the North Island decided that the best way to protect their territory would be to unite under one leader. In 1858 they chose the Waikato chief Potatau Te Wherowhero as their king. They declared their lands *tapu*

Courtesy of New Zealand Tourist and Publicity Office

Built in 1831, the Mission House at Waimate North was part of the first inland mission in New Zealand. Here, Church of England missionaries taught farming methods to the Maori. In the churchyard lie soldiers killed in the 1845 Bay of Islands uprising.

29

(sacred) and placed them under the king's protection.

Governor Gore Browne, Grey's successor, considered the election of a Maori king illegal. He also decided that the colonists and the Maori would have to settle their differences by force. A dispute over land in Taranaki in 1860 became violent and triggered the Land Wars—a series of confrontations between some Maori groups and the British that lasted until 1872.

The British had difficulty subduing the Maori resisters because they knew the terrain and were skilled warriors. Eventually, however, disease and the greater strength of the British forces weakened the Maori fighters. They withdrew to an area known as the King Country, between the Taranaki and Waikato regions. During the conflicts, the government seized about three million acres of Maori land, half of which it sold to help pay the cost of the battles. The other half was later returned to the Maori.

Economic Changes

To be closer to the more populated South Island, the government moved the capital from Auckland to Wellington—on the southern tip of the North Island—in 1865. A few years earlier, prospectors had discovered gold on the South Island. The find caused an economic boom that drew many immigrants to the country. But the gold dwindled after the middle of the decade, leaving thousands of people with no work. The cost of fighting the Land Wars added to New Zealand's hardships. And when prices for its main exports—wool and wheat—fell in the late 1860s, the country faced serious economic problems.

Photo by Hocken Library, University of Otago, Dunedin

During the 1880s, most Maori lived in small rural villages and had little contact with British settlers. These Maori lived at Koriniti, a village on the Wanganui River, which flows south from Mount Taranaki.

Many rural Maori farmed on a small scale in the late 1800s. These women, who lived north of Auckland, are harvesting *kumaras,* one of the starchy roots that enabled the early Maori in New Zealand to survive.

In 1870 New Zealand's treasurer, Julius Vogel, proposed a solution to these problems through a program to create jobs and develop the country at the same time. The government borrowed $40 million to construct railways, roads, bridges, telegraph lines, and government buildings. Railroads opened interior areas of the North Island,

and settlers cleared hillsides for agriculture. Trains carried meat, wool, grain, and dairy products to ports for shipment on new steamship lines.

The transportation networks simplified travel within the country and aided the development of manufacturing. Factories produced woolen cloth, farm machinery, and

An abandoned gold-mining dredge on the South Island's western coast is left over from the gold rush days of the 1860s. By the late 1800s, New Zealand was exporting dredges and other mining equipment.

The Kingston Flyer, a restored nineteenth-century locomotive, crosses a river in central Otago. As part of the government's public-works policy, New Zealand constructed many railroad lines in the 1870s. Steam engines were built in Dunedin.

refrigeration and mining equipment. By paying low wages, New Zealand's manufacturers could sell their goods abroad despite the high cost of shipping to distant places.

Freezing and refrigeration came into use on ships during the 1880s. The first cargo of frozen meat sent to Great Britain in 1882 earned a considerable profit for New Zealand farmers. The success of this technology made them less dependent on wool and wheat for income. Refrigeration also meant cheese and butter could withstand the long trip to Europe. As a result, more people wanted to become dairy farmers. They pressured the government to make small farms available, since dairying could be done on a small scale. In 1886 the government broke up a few large estates and settled some poor families on the land.

Social Reforms

Despite improvements in transportation and manufacturing, however, New Zea-land experienced severe economic problems throughout the 1880s. Prices for wool and grain exports remained low. Unemployed farm workers could not find jobs in factories. Thousands of immigrants who had come during the gold rush left New Zealand.

As poverty spread, unemployed workers demanded legislation that would improve living conditions. Many New Zealanders wanted the government to provide land for more farms. Others called for laws to regulate working conditions, especially in places employing women and children.

The newly formed Liberal party won a majority of House seats in 1890 and responded to these demands. Under John Ballance and his successor, Richard Seddon, the Liberals enacted sweeping social reforms. The government created more than 5,000 new farms. It passed the Land and Income Tax Act, which forced many wealthy property owners to sell parts of their estates to pay their taxes.

Mount Tarawera erupted in June 1886, killing more than 100 people as it spewed rock, lava, and ash over a 6,000-square-mile area. The volcano buried three villages and the nearby pink and white mineral terraces—geologic formations that were much admired by nineteenth-century tourists and writers.

Richard John Seddon *(right)*, New Zealand's prime minister from 1893 to 1906, and his wife *(second from left)* met with the king and queen of Raratonga on a visit to the Cook Islands. New Zealand administered the Cook Islands from 1888 until 1965, when the Cook Islands became self-governing.

New Zealand troops parade for onlookers before departing for Europe during World War I (1914–1918). The anniversary of their landing on Turkey's Gallipoli Peninsula on April 25, 1915, is observed each year as a national holiday—Anzac Day. New Zealand sent more than 100,000 troops overseas to help Britain and its allies defeat Germany.

New laws gave employees bargaining rights and protected women and children from long working hours and unsafe conditions in factories and shops. In 1893 New Zealand became the first nation to give voting rights to women. That same year, the government extended free education from the primary to the secondary level. In 1898 the country passed a plan to provide payments (pensions) to the elderly. By the turn of the century, New Zealanders benefited from some of the world's most advanced social programs.

In 1907 Britain granted the colony status as a dominion—a self-governing country within the British Empire. When World War I broke out in 1914, New Zealand sided with Britain against Germany. The

New Zealand was a prosperous country in the early twentieth century. Mona Vale, in Christchurch, was the home of Annie Townend, one of the nation's wealthiest women. She inherited a fortune from her father, a prosperous sheep rancher.

dominion sent more than 100,000 troops to Europe and Africa. Called Anzacs, they fought in the Australian and New Zealand Army Corps. By the war's end in 1918, 17,000 New Zealanders had died as a result of the fighting.

The 1930s and 1940s

After the war and throughout the 1920s, New Zealand developed its agriculture and industry, and living conditions continued to improve. In the 1930s, however, New Zealand's economy suffered from the effects of a worldwide economic depression. Prices for agricultural exports dropped, and thousands of people lost their jobs. Most workers had to take pay cuts. In addition, the nation could not afford to maintain many of its social programs, so it reduced spending on health services, pensions, education, and public works.

In 1935, the Labour party came to power. Led by Michael Savage, the Labour government began to increase spending in order to create jobs. It also set up a broad government insurance system. This program included pension coverage for the elderly, the disabled, widows, and orphans. It also paid most medical costs for citizens.

The government guaranteed farmers minimum prices for their products and built houses for workers. It cut the work week from 44 to 40 hours. Between 1936 and 1946, the Labour party strengthened New Zealand as a welfare state—a country in which the government takes responsibility for the well-being of its citizens.

In the 1930s, as part of its economic recovery, New Zealand became less dependent on Great Britain by developing more industries and by establishing its own unit of money and a central bank. Nevertheless, when Britain declared war on Nazi Germany in 1939, New Zealand quickly did the same. About 140,000 New Zealand soldiers served with British and Allied troops during World War II (1939–1945).

Photo by Hocken Library, University of Otago, Dunedin

Maui Pomare, a Maori physician, started a medical and sanitation program that helped the Maori to improve their health and to increase their numbers in the early 1900s. Pomare later served in New Zealand's Parliament.

Courtesy of New Zealand Herald

Elected prime minister in 1935, Michael Savage led the movement to establish a full-scale social security system and comprehensive health care in New Zealand. His policies helped revive the country's depressed economy.

Troops of a Maori battalion prepare to leave for Italy during World War II (1939-1945).

More than 11,800 New Zealanders lost their lives in the conflict against Germany, Italy, and Japan, and an additional 15,700 suffered injuries.

The wartime battles in Asia helped New Zealanders realize that their country's past ties to Britain could not guarantee their security in the South Pacific. As a result, in 1944 New Zealand signed the Canberra Pact, which strengthened relations with Australia. New Zealand also formed a strong alliance with the United States, which had used the country as a base of operations against Japan during the war. In 1945 New Zealand joined the United Nations as a founding member.

New Zealand formally gained full independence from Great Britain in 1947 under the Statute of Westminster. The new nation became a member of the British Commonwealth (an organization that includes Britain and its former colonies). New Zealand also entered into two defense agreements. The ANZUS Treaty (with the United States and Australia) and the Southeast Asia Treaty Organization (SEATO) both sought to maintain peace in the South Pacific.

Postwar Developments

Along with responsibilities in international affairs, New Zealand was faced with domestic changes and concerns. A postwar economic boom expanded industrial production and created new jobs. Many Maori, pakehas, and Pacific Islanders moved to the thriving Auckland area to work. In the 1960s and 1970s, environmentalists promoted conservation of natural resources.

Courtesy of Baptist Mid-Missions

Workers finished Auckland Harbour Bridge in 1959, a time of rapid population growth in the Auckland area.

Courtesy of New Zealand Tourist and Publicity Office

The huge Kinleith Paper Mill at Tokoroa on the Volcanic Plateau employs 4,500 people. In the 1960s, New Zealand's output of paper and other timber products expanded rapidly. Paper and wood-pulp facilities created many jobs but also added pollutants to air, water, and soil.

Boats carrying protesters surrounded a U.S. Navy nuclear submarine in Auckland's harbor in 1984. New Zealand has since banned nuclear-powered ships and vessels containing nuclear weapons from its waters.

Courtesy of New Zealand Herald

These activists opposed both nuclear testing and the admission of nuclear-equipped ships into New Zealand ports.

Except for one three-year period, the National party, which was first organized in the 1930s, ran the government from 1949 to 1972. In 1972 the Labour party won a majority of seats in the House of Representatives. Party leader Norman Kirk soon faced an economic crisis.

In 1973 Britain—New Zealand's main trading partner—joined the European Community (EC). This organization required Britain to limit purchases of agricultural goods produced outside the EC. As a result, Britain sharply cut imports from New Zealand, and many New Zealanders lost their jobs. Adding to the economic crisis were rising prices for oil and other imported goods.

As conditions worsened, voters in 1975 again elected the National party. Under the leadership of Robert Muldoon, the government tightened controls on wages, prices, immigration, and imports. Muldoon also increased public borrowing and spending—a method that had helped New Zealand recover from past crises. This time, however, the strategy failed and economic problems grew. Muldoon's administration also had to deal with tensions between the Maori and pakeha populations.

Recent Events

Voters elected the National party again in 1978 and 1981, showing their support for its policies. But the country's economy remained weak, and the Labour party won a majority of seats in the House of Representatives in 1984, making David Lange the country's prime minister.

After taking office, Lange strengthened New Zealand's opposition to nuclear weapons and nuclear power. Ships and submarines powered by nuclear reactors or any vessel carrying nuclear weapons could not enter New Zealand's waters. This policy meant that military vessels from the United States, one of New Zealand's partners in the ANZUS Treaty, could not use New Zealand's ports. The government maintained its position, however, and the ANZUS group has not met since 1984.

Meanwhile, the country's weak economy caused high unemployment and inflation (rising prices). Lange's government tried to improve conditions by lowering income taxes, which had been the country's main source of income, and by raising taxes on goods and services. Because these changes would hurt the poor, the government also increased payments to lower-income families.

Other economic policies also changed. Although most businesses were already privately owned, the government was involved in much of the country's economic activity. For years the government had helped keep farmers in business with subsidies (payments) and had placed tariffs (taxes) on imported goods to protect industries in New Zealand from foreign competition. Lange believed subsidies and tariffs hurt the economy and reduced them to improve trade with other countries.

Most New Zealanders agreed that the changes were necessary, but for a while the new policies made things even worse. Farmers lost their land, manufacturing businesses failed, and unemployment rose to 11 percent. At one point, the country's population declined as people moved away

Courtesy of the Office of the Prime Minister, Wellington

Jim Bolger, the leader of New Zealand's National party, was elected prime minister in 1990 and reelected in 1993.

from New Zealand to find work. The economy was still weak in 1990, and frustrated voters brought the National party back to power that year.

Under the new government of Jim Bolger, the country's economy began to recover and living conditions improved. The government now plays a smaller role in business and in social issues, providing fewer services for New Zealanders. It remains to be seen how well the Bolger government's policies will address the country's economic concerns over the long term.

Government

New Zealand is an independent nation in the British Commonwealth, and its government is closely patterned after Britain's. Its constitution is not a single document but rather consists of many laws passed by Parliament and important rulings by the courts. The governor-general—whose role

Courtesy of the Office of the Prime Minister, Wellington

David Lange took a strong stand against nuclear weapons soon after becoming prime minister in 1984.

is ceremonial—represents the British monarch, the symbolic ruler of New Zealand.

Executive authority rests with the prime minister and the cabinet, which usually has about 20 members. The prime minister is the leader of the party that holds the most seats in the House of Representatives, which is the only chamber in the Parliament. All cabinet ministers are chosen from the governing party's members in the House. Each cabinet official administers several departments of government. In a referendum (a special election) in 1993, voters changed the way members of parliament are elected and how Parliament works.

Legislative authority lies with the House of Representatives, which in 1994 had 120 seats—64 for candidates elected directly and 56 for members chosen by political parties. If the majority party has fewer than 60 seats, it may join with another party to form a government. All citizens 18 years of age or older must register to vote, and voter turnout during elections is very high. Maori candidates and voters can register on Maori electoral rolls or in the general electorate.

The legislature meets between June and November to propose, debate, and either pass or reject laws. Parliamentary elections normally occur every three years, although the prime minister can call an election sooner if the House does not agree with the administration on a major issue.

The highest judicial body in New Zealand is the Court of Appeals. Decisions of that court are final unless parties obtain permission to take their cases to Great Britain's Privy Council. Cases reach the top court from a lower appeals court called the High Court. The nation's principal trial courts are the district courts.

Because it is small in area, New Zealand has been able to develop a strong central government with most of the responsibility for running the country resting with government officials in Wellington. More than 100 county governments provide for the needs of rural populations. Governmental units in cities and towns also handle local matters.

The flag (ensign) of New Zealand was adopted in 1901. The British flag, symbolic of New Zealand's historic link to Great Britain, occupies the top left-hand corner. Against a blue field on the right half of the flag is the Southern Cross, a constellation visible in the Southern Hemisphere. Occasions on which many New Zealanders fly the ensign include New Zealand Day (February 6), Anzac Day (April 25), and the actual and official birthdays of the country's monarch.

Artwork by Laura Westlund

Photo by Emily Slowinski

Children play at a summer social gathering in January near Christchurch on the South Island. Living in a country that provides a high level of social services, New Zealand children receive free medical and dental care and free education.

3) The People

About three-fourths of New Zealand's 3.5 million people live on the North Island, mainly in urban areas on the coasts and lower hills. For nearly 20 years, the nation experienced high unemployment. As a result, the government has restricted immigration primarily to persons with skills that the country needs. Because jobs are scarce, many young, well-educated New Zealanders leave their homeland to find jobs in Australia.

During some years in the 1980s, more people left New Zealand than moved in. The population is still increasing, however, because of a sufficiently high birthrate. But emigration reduces the growth rate, which was less than 1 percent in 1990. At that level of expansion, the population will double in 81 years.

Persons of European descent make up 82 percent of New Zealand's people. Another 12 percent of the population are Maori, and 4 percent are Polynesians. Included in the remaining 2 percent of the nation's residents are people with Chinese, East Indian, and Southeast Asian backgrounds. New Zealand's Maori and Polynesian populations are growing most rapidly.

Shoppers and office workers walk along Lambton Quay, the main commercial street in Wellington. This street once ran along the waterfront. In recent years, however, city developers have reclaimed land from the harbor, and now Lambton Quay is several blocks from the water.

Courtesy of New Zealand Tourist and Publicity Office

Ethnic Mixture

Ninety percent of New Zealanders with European ancestry trace their family origins to Great Britain. This heritage that most New Zealanders share is reflected in their customs, family ties, and language. Most British settlers were working- or middle-class immigrants from England and Scotland, but a small number came from Ireland. These British immigrants adopted an attitude of equality in social matters and favored a community approach to solving problems.

The strong link to Great Britain has influenced the course of New Zealand's history, but ties are loosening, and the expression "old country" in reference to Britain is becoming less common. Many neighborhoods still look very British. Now, however, cities are reflecting the influence of Maori and North American cultures on New Zealand's way of life.

After World War II, the Maori began moving from rural areas to urban centers —particularly Auckland—to find jobs. By the 1980s, 90 percent of the Maori lived in cities. The change in lifestyle caused problems for many Maori, who had been accustomed to living with extended families in close-knit communities. Because their rural schools had prepared the Maori for an agricultural way of life, most of them lacked the broad educational background needed to obtain good jobs. Some pakeha property owners refused to rent to Maori tenants.

Pressing their noses together, these Maori women greet each other with a *hongi,* the formal Maori welcome. In traditional Maori belief, two people intermingle their *hau* (spirit) when they perform the hongi.

Although many Maori and pakehas have intermarried, tensions between the two groups have increased in recent years. The Maori, who have lower incomes and a shorter life expectancy than pakehas, have a higher rate of unemployment.

A small but vocal group of Maori activists is demanding that the government settle long-standing disputes over land-ownership. Their claims, based on the Treaty of Waitangi, assert that many pakehas are holding illegal titles to land and that such properties should be returned to the Maori. Some Maori have conducted angry protests in recent years to make their point.

Although urban living has not been easy for all Maori, it has made their own unique

Mount Taranaki forms the backdrop for this elementary school on the North Island. The building, with walk-through classrooms and large windows, is typical of New Zealand's newer schools.

culture—called *Maoritanga*—visible to more New Zealanders. Some Maori who were brought up to speak only English are also learning Maori, an official language of New Zealand. At special centers, young and old are studying the traditional arts of their people—weaving, carving, singing, dancing, and storytelling.

Maori community life still centers on the *marae*—an open area of land with a community building for eating and sleeping—where social, political, and ceremonial events take place. Some urban Maori return to their ancestral marae on special occasions, but others now attend meeting halls that have been built in cities. These new marae have successfully adapted traditional ways to modern circumstances.

Non-Maori Polynesians began immigrating to New Zealand in the mid-1800s, when missionaries brought them to the country for religious training. After World War II, the rate of this migration—mostly from Western Samoa and the Cook Islands—increased. The Pacific Islanders do not all share the same culture and language. Some groups have chosen to preserve their customs and pass them on to their children.

Like the Maori, some Pacific Islanders have struggled against discrimination in housing and job opportunities. Many have had to accept low-paying jobs. Others have achieved considerable economic success.

Daily Life and Religion

New Zealanders share their land with almost 70 million sheep, but only a small number of people live on large sheep stations (ranches). On small farms, mechanization

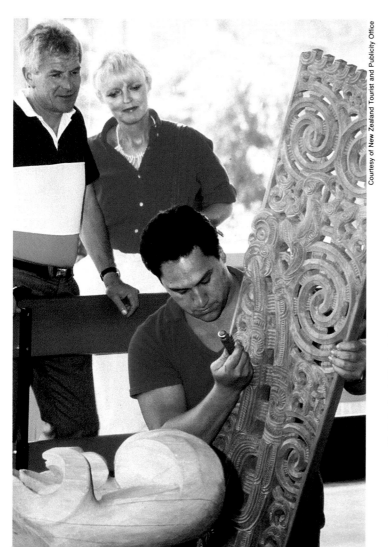

At a school in Rotorua, a Maori woodcarver carries on an age-old art form. Two early twentieth-century Maori leaders—Sir Apirana Ngata and Sir Peter Buck—headed the movement to revive Maori culture. Through their efforts, traditional meeting houses came to be used as schools where the Maori could learn carving, weaving, and other historic arts.

Fans watch a cricket match at the Basin Reserve in Wellington. Cricket, a bat-and-ball game developed in Great Britain, is the most popular summer sport in New Zealand.

Most New Zealanders live in single-family homes with large yards. For many, flower gardening is a favorite pastime.

45

has decreased the need for workers. As a result, farming employs only 9.7 percent of the total labor force. Most New Zealanders hold jobs in the service sector, commerce, manufacturing, agriculture, finance, communications, fishing, forestry, and construction. They usually work a five-day, 40-hour week.

The majority of the country's citizens enjoy a comfortable standard of living, although in times of economic hardship, some families live in poverty. Government services and welfare benefits assist low-income New Zealanders, however. Most families own an automobile and their own home. Rivers, lakes, seacoasts, and mountains provide many recreational opportunities within easy reach of most people.

Churches do not exert a great influence in New Zealand, and religious matters are strictly separated from the state. Most pakehas and Maori belong to the Christian faith. The leading Christian congregations in the country are Anglican (Church of England), Presbyterian, Roman Catholic, and Methodist.

Trainees from other countries in the South Pacific come to New Zealand to study administration, public service, and economic development. Here, a young man from Western Samoa *(standing)* works with a New Zealander in a government office. Western Samoa, a former New Zealand trusteeship, became independent in 1962.

Girls play in the surf at Birdlings Flat near Christchurch. New Zealanders live only a short distance from the ocean, and easy access to beaches, rivers and mountains enhances their quality of life.

46

Students dressed in school blazers leave their classes at a private school in Christchurch. Only 3 percent of New Zealand children attend private schools, most of which are run by Christian churches.

Welfare and Education

New Zealand's government has a long history of providing public services, from free education to retirement pensions. Support is available for accident victims, the sick or injured, the disabled, the unemployed, and unmarried parents. These services help New Zealanders maintain an adequate standard of living.

Most medical expenses are paid by national health insurance, provided by the government. The government covers a large portion of doctors' fees and part of the cost of treatment in private hospitals. Children and teenagers receive free dental care. The quality of health care is reflected in a low infant death rate (7 deaths per 1,000 live births) and a high average life expectancy—76 years.

Virtually all New Zealanders can read and write. Most children in New Zealand begin school at age 5, and attendance is required for ages 6 through 16. Education is free through age 19. Many children 3 to 5 years of age attend play centers, which the government partially funds. Students who live in remote areas can take cor-respondence courses that are broadcast over radio stations. Secondary school graduates who pass a national examination can attend one of seven universities, whose total enrollment is nearly 90,000 students. Community colleges, technical institutes, and adult programs provide additional educational opportunities.

Art and Literature

During centuries of isolation from other peoples, the Maori applied their artistic talent to the wood, stones, flax, and other materials of New Zealand, developing unique art forms and designs. Carving was the art of men, and weaving was the art of women. Both forms decorated meeting houses and the homes of important people. Modern Maori carry on the artistic traditions of their people, but the best—such as sculptor Arnold Wilson and painter Ralph Hotere—do not just duplicate works of the past. They blend their own ideas with old styles, creating new Maori art.

Pakeha art and literature developed slowly. Early in this century, some New

47

A carver uses an electric instrument to polish a *tiki* (human form) from greenstone (New Zealand jade). Before Europeans arrived with metal tools, greenstone was one of the most valuable materials the Maori possessed. They used the hard stone as a tool to till the soil and carve wood. Using water and sandstone, they patiently shaped the substance into ornaments and weapons. The Maori treasured greenstone tikis, objects that represented their ancestors.

Photo by David Bateman Ltd.

Zealand writers and artists traveled to Europe to work. Among these was Katherine Mansfield, who began publishing her short stories after moving to Britain in 1906 at the age of 19. The painter Frances Hodgkins also left her homeland to work in Europe, where she first won recognition. Although Dame Ngaio Marsh lived most of her life in New Zealand, this mystery writer's most famous novels concern a British detective.

In the 1930s, works reflecting New Zealand's own distinctive culture began to emerge. Leading this movement were some pakeha poets—A. R. D. Fairburn, Robin Hyde, Allen Curnow, and James K. Baxter. Using his poetry to express social issues, Baxter lived the last part of his life in a Maori community.

The popular writer Frank Sargeson wrote many stories and novels about New Zealand but died in poverty near Auckland. Janet Frame, one of New Zealand's greatest novelists, earned an international reputation for her many novels and stories but found it difficult to earn a living as an author in such a small country. Maurice Shadbolt, known primarily for his fiction, has written several nonfiction accounts of New Zealand.

A growing number of Maori writers are expressing in English what it means to be Maori in pakeha society. Notable among these authors is Keri Hulme, whose novel *The Bone People* won Britain's top literary award—the Booker Prize—in 1986.

New Zealand painters have found inspiration in local surroundings. Charles

Heaphy, a soldier and surveyor who arrived in New Zealand in 1840, became the country's first great painter. Colin McCahon, perhaps the nation's most famous artist, painted landscapes that reflected his own visions. Peter McIntyre's landscapes realistically portray the New Zealand countryside and are very popular. Gordon Walters uses the coiled shape of a young fern leaf—which also inspired Maori carvers—as a dominant design in his abstract paintings.

Recreation and Sports

New Zealanders are sports enthusiasts—both as participants and spectators. Rugby, a type of football, ranks as the most popular sport. The national team—the All Blacks, which takes its name from its black uniforms—plays international matches between June and September. Local rugby leagues are also popular.

During summer, most fans devote their attention to cricket—a bat-and-ball game developed in Britain involving two 11-member teams. Teams from overseas arrive in February and March to compete against New Zealand's best players. Soccer is also popular, both with amateurs and professional athletes, who compete in tournaments at home and abroad. Hockey teams also meet competitors from other countries. Netball—a game similar to basketball—is a major women's sport played outdoors in winter. International netball tournaments take place in May and June.

New Zealand's athletes have excelled in world competition. They earned 10 medals in the 1992 Summer Olympics for boxing, cycling, track and field, equestrian events, swimming, and yachting and one in the Winter Olympics for women's slalom skiing. New Zealand has also produced outstanding runners. Competing in Sweden in 1975, John Walker became the first person to run a mile in less than 3 minutes, 50 seconds. Another New Zealander, Sir Edmund Hillary, was the first person to climb to the top of Nepal's Mount Everest, the world's tallest peak.

The yacht *New Zealand* challenged the U.S. boat *Stars and Stripes* for the America's Cup racing trophy in 1988. The New Zealand lost the race then won the trophy when the *Stars and Stripes* was disqualified and finally lost again when the U.S. team won the cup back in court. New Zealand's yachting team fought back in competition and won the America's Cup with the yacht *Black Magic 1* in 1995.

Photo by Reuters/Bettmann Newsphotos

49

Rugby—the game from which U.S. football originated—is New Zealand's favorite spectator sport. Because players do not wear pads, they can run very fast. International matches are scheduled between June and September. The season for nonprofessional rugby (called club rugby) begins in April.

New Zealand's natural features lend themselves to recreational sports, including white-water rafting and canoeing, sailing, camping, skiing, and tramping (the New Zealand word for hiking). The country's lakes, rivers, and coastal waters at-tract fishermen from throughout the world. Horse racing is a popular spectator sport, and New Zealand breeders raise some of the world's finest horses. Many rural New Zealanders who own horses play a rugged version of polo.

A curious horse checks supplies while an artist paints the alps near Arrowtown in Otago on the South Island.

Although the missionary Samuel Marsden brought the first grapevines to New Zealand in 1819, wine making has only recently become an important industry. The country's wines have earned a reputation for quality in foreign markets as well as locally. These vines are growing in Upper Moutere, in the northeastern area of the South Island.

Photo by Ted Scott

4) The Economy

Land is New Zealand's most important economic resource. The country depends on trade to sell its large agricultural output and to obtain the raw materials and manufactured goods it lacks. For many decades, Great Britain bought most of New Zealand's meat, wool, and dairy products. Trade with Britain declined sharply in the early 1970s, however, when that nation joined the European Community and began exchanging more goods with other members of that organization.

Since then, Europe, Australia, Japan, and the United States have been New Zea-land's leading trading partners. However, South Korea, China, and other countries of the Middle East and eastern Asia are increasingly important customers. In addition, New Zealand and Australia have signed a contract called the Closer Economic Relations Trade Agreement, which eliminates import taxes on goods sold by one country to the other.

While seeking new markets, New Zealand has also worked to offer more types of goods to foreign buyers. Meat, wool, and dairy products are still the country's leading exports, providing much of

An orchard worker picks one of New Zealand's most famous products—the kiwifruit. Originally known as the Chinese gooseberry, the imported plants thrived in New Zealand, where growers selectively cultivated the vines and eventually produced larger, tastier fruit.

Hereford cattle graze on the South Island. To utilize pasture more fully, farmers often raise beef cattle and sheep on the same land. Selective breeding has made New Zealand's beef herds among the best in the world.

the nation's foreign earnings. But tourism, manufactured goods, fish, and timber products are growing sources of income from abroad.

Agriculture

About 55 percent of New Zealand's land area is used for agriculture. The higher hills provide pasture for hardy sheep, and farms on lower hills and flatlands raise cattle, sheep, and other livestock. Only 3 percent of the farmland is cultivated for crops.

A mild climate allows sheep and cattle to graze year-round in most areas of the country. To be productive, however, grasslands require heavy applications of chemical fertilizer. Because much of the terrain is too steep for tractors, farmers spread fertilizer and grass seed on their pastures from airplanes and helicopters.

Although a few sheep stations cover thousands of acres, most of New Zealand's farms are small. Many farmers are raising more types of animals to protect themselves when prices for wool, meat, and dairy products are low. Beef cattle, goats, and deer supplement dairy cattle and sheep on a number of farms. Goats furnish milk, meat, and a kind of wool called mohair. Red deer provide venison (deer meat) and hides for export. Some farmers are devoting more land to cultivating fruits—including apples, kiwifruit, apricots, boysenberries, peaches, and pears.

SHEEP FARMING

New Zealand is the world's largest supplier of lamb and mutton and, after Australia, the second largest exporter of wool.

About 90 percent of the country's raw wool is sold abroad. In addition to meat and wool, sheep provide sausage casings, skins, and tallow (fat).

With 24,000 farms raising sheep as their main product, these animals outnumber people in New Zealand 20 to 1. The average flock contains about 1,800 head, but some of the large stations in the high country of the South Island support 20,000 animals. The smaller sheep farms are family-run operations that employ outside help for seasonal tasks. Traveling groups of shearers usually clip the sheep. A good shearer can shave more than 300 animals per day. In the high country, shepherds patrol large flocks on motorized trail bikes and rely on dogs to help handle the flocks efficiently.

The Romney breed of sheep, to which the majority of present-day flocks in New Zealand belong, has a coarse wool that is ideal for carpet making.

Professional shearers travel from farm to farm to clip sheep, each worker cutting the wool from about 300 sheep a day. A bale of wool, which weighs about 340 pounds, contains fleeces from about four dozen sheep.

DAIRY AND BEEF CATTLE

New Zealand has more than three million dairy cattle. Dairy farms, which average 100 acres in size, lie mostly in the Waikato and Taranaki areas of the North Island. New Zealand farmers pioneered the use of mechanical milkers, and advanced equipment keeps them among the most efficient dairy producers in the world.

About 13 percent of the milk is either consumed fresh or fed to livestock. Factories convert the rest into butter, cheese, skim- and whole-milk powders, and other products. Like many agricultural goods in New Zealand, these are sold through a cooperative organization. The New Zealand Dairy Board acquires the items from manufacturers and markets them abroad.

For many years farmers kept beef cattle primarily to trample down unwanted plants in pastures. Although the animals still perform that service, 4.5 million cattle are now raised primarily for their meat. The beef sold for export is boned, cut, wrapped, and shipped in cartons to the United States and Canada.

CROP FARMING

Although New Zealand grows most of its own food, it does import coffee, tea, sugar, beverages, spices, and some fruits and vegetables. Barley is an important export crop. The country grows sufficient wheat, corn, peas, and potatoes to meet most of its needs. Leading fruit exports include apples, citrus species, nectarines, peaches, berries, avocados, and kiwifruit. Local vineyards grow grapes for making wine. Some of these new wineries have gained international reputations.

Courtesy of Richard Southward

Cattle graze year-round in many regions, heading twice a day toward milking sheds. Many of the sheds are equipped with computer-controlled mechanical milkers. New Zealand's milk production per dairy farmer is the highest in the world because of the country's moderate climate, its nutritious grasses, and farmer-scientist cooperation.

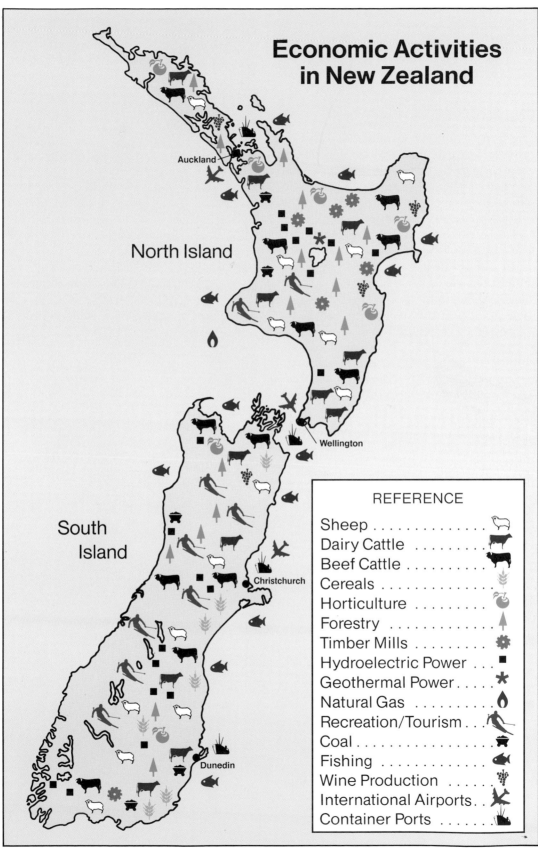

Economic Activities in New Zealand

North Island

South Island

Auckland

Wellington

Christchurch

Dunedin

REFERENCE

Sheep . . . .
Dairy Cattle . . . .
Beef Cattle . . . .
Cereals . . . .
Horticulture . . . .
Forestry . . . .
Timber Mills . . . .
Hydroelectric Power . . .
Geothermal Power . . . . .
Natural Gas . . . .
Recreation/Tourism . . .
Coal . . . .
Fishing . . . .
Wine Production . . . . . .
International Airports . .
Container Ports . . . . . .

Artwork by Laura Westlund

A truck carries logs to a sawmill through forests of planted pine trees on the Volcanic Plateau. New Zealand's timber harvests will increase substantially in the years ahead.

Forestry and Fishing

The forestry industry, one of the fastest growing parts of New Zealand's economy, uses 15 percent of the nation's land. Radiata pines—the main tree crop—thrive in plantations on the Volcanic Plateau, the center of timber production. Douglas fir and native evergreens, such as rimu, also provide a small amount of timber. Forestry management programs, which plant new trees for future harvests, ensure that timber supplies will continue to be available.

Forestry industries, which now earn 8 percent of the country's export income, employ 10 percent of the entire manufacturing work force. The boom in wood products has stimulated businesses that serve

Workers can learn logging skills—such as operating this giant crane—at the Forestry Training Center in Rotorua.

the forestry sector, such as transport, vehicle repair, and construction. Pulp and paper companies turn out newsprint, paper, paperboard, wood panels, plywood, and particle board. Australia, Japan, Hong Kong, and South Korea purchase most of New Zealand's wood products and timber.

Fishing is also of increasing importance to New Zealand's economy. In 1978 the government began policing a 200-mile Exclusive Economic Zone (EEZ) around the country's coasts to control fishing activities by other nations' vessels. The establishment of the EEZ encouraged New Zealand's commercial fishermen, who had concentrated mainly on shallow coastal waters, to invest in larger, deepwater vessels. As a result, the country's fishing industry expanded rapidly in the 1980s. Nelson, on the northern coast of the South Island, is the nation's busiest fishing port.

New Zealand exports most of its annual catch to Japan, Australia, and the United States. The major hauls include hoki, jack mackerel, orange roughy, snapper, and barracouta. Rock lobster is a valuable coastal resource, and oysters, scallops, and mussels are important shellfish. Salmon farming is a growing source of income. Trout, whitebait, and other freshwater species help the economy mainly by attracting sport fishermen to New Zealand from throughout the world.

Mining and Manufacturing

Although New Zealand does not contain a lot of minerals, it does have abundant amounts of coal as well as deposits of sand that yield iron ore. Large supplies of phosphorite, which is used to make fertilizer, also exist. Sands rich in iron are mined on the North Island's western coast. The iron is sold to domestic and foreign steel manufacturers.

Coal currently meets 9 percent of the nation's energy needs. The country expects to mine increasing amounts of the mineral as it moves toward self-sufficiency

Photo by Emily Slowinski

With Mitre Peak for a backdrop, fishing boats cling to a dock in Fiordland's Milford Sound on the South Island.

Independent Picture Service

A Maori fisherman looks well pleased with his catch of lobster. New Zealand exports lobster to the United States.

57

At the Wairakei Thermal Power Station on the Volcanic Plateau, underground steam is tapped and used to power turbines that generate electricity. The plant has been operating since 1954.

Photo by Ted Scott

in energy production. Hydropower stations provide the bulk of New Zealand's electricity. In some parts of the Volcanic Plateau, pockets of steam in the earth's crust are tapped to provide heat for homes and businesses and to power a paper mill.

New Zealand must import nearly all the petroleum it uses. As a result, increases in world oil prices can hurt the country's economy. The nation does have large supplies of natural gas, however, in the Kapuni field in Taranaki and in the offshore Maui field. Much of this resource is converted into synthetic gasoline and methanol to supply about 50 percent of the nation's transportation fuel. Some of the gas is used to generate electricity, and some is converted into chemicals. The nation's one oil refinery recently expanded.

Manufacturing is an important part of New Zealand's economy. In addition to its other exported goods, New Zealand sells machinery and metals to other countries. The country's factories provide an increasing range of industrial and consumer goods. Two companies produce steel, but New Zealand imports stainless steel to make equipment for the dairy, brewery, chemical, and forestry industries. A large facility at Bluff, on the South Island, makes aluminum for Asian markets.

A number of plants in New Zealand assemble motor vehicles—mostly of Japanese origin. Other companies produce ships, tugs, barges, trawlers, and yachts. The plastics and textile industries manufacture a variety of consumer goods. Makers of leather goods and woolen carpets and textiles have abundant supplies of raw materials, and their products are major export items.

Transportation

Despite its rugged terrain, New Zealand has an excellent highway system that includes more than 58,000 miles of roads. Building this network required the construction of many bridges and tunnels—some a mile long. Rains and washouts take a heavy toll on the country's roads, about half of which are paved. Many are surfaced with gravel so that they can be easily repaired when major disruptions occur.

A railway system links New Zealand's main cities, using nearly 1,600 miles of track on the North Island and 1,065 on the South Island. The New Zealand Railways Corporation operates both freight and passenger services. The company's operating equipment and trains are very modern. The main lines for passenger service connect Auckland and Wellington on the

Photo by Emily Slowinski

A very winding road *(left)* runs from Queenstown 17 miles north to Skippers. The route passes through an area where rich gold deposits were found during the 1860s. Travelers *(below)* study their car to see if it can squeeze past a truck that has broken down on the Skippers Road.

Photo by Emily Slowinski

59

A Cook Strait ferry bound for Wellington passes another boat heading for Picton. The New Zealand Railways Corporation operates the ferry service, which takes passengers, automobiles, and railroad cars between New Zealand's main islands. Up-to-date trains *(left)* carry travelers between cities.

North Island and Christchurch and Invercargill on the South Island. Two ferries carry vehicles and passengers, as well as railway cars, across Cook Strait from Wellington to Picton.

Air New Zealand—which is partly owned by Australia's Qantas Airlines—provides international and domestic air service. Many other carriers also provide service to international airports in Auckland, Christchurch, and Wellington. The New Zealand Line sends cargo ships to Europe, Japan, South Korea, Australia, the South Pacific, and North America. Vessels from other nations, however, carry most goods shipped from New Zealand's ports. The largest cargo ports are Auckland and Wellington on the North Island and Lyttleton (which serves Christchurch) and Port Chalmers (at Dunedin) on the South Island.

Tourism

The tourism industry has grown rapidly in recent years, providing the country's largest single source of foreign income. Since 1988, more than a million visitors from other countries have come to New Zealand every year. The greatest number of foreign travelers come from Australia, followed by the United States, Japan, and Great Britain. Several new resorts have been built to accommodate them.

Many tourists are attracted by New Zealand's natural beauty, its unusual geothermal features, and its unpolluted environment. Recreation-minded travelers take advantage of opportunities for skiing, tramping, rafting, fishing, and other outdoor activities. Other visitors are interested in observing New Zealand's multicultural society and its progressive agricultural industries.

Courtesy of New Zealand Tourist and Publicity Office

Skiers enjoy the slopes of Mount Hutt in the Southern Alps. Skiing attracts many vacationers to New Zealand.

Courtesy of New Zealand Tourist and Publicity Office

Waitomo Cave south of Hamilton contains millions of glowworms. These larvae of a New Zealand fly release sticky, shimmering threads to attract the insects they eat. The glowing tails of the larvae create an interesting sight for visitors.

New Zealanders travel frequently, taking regular vacations as part of their lifestyle. Ten national parks, which cover about 12 percent of the country's land area, draw domestic, as well as foreign, vacationers. The biggest in area—and one of the largest national parks in the world—is Fiordland National Park. This preserve, in the southwestern corner of the South Island, is known for its fiords, snow-capped mountains, forests, waterfalls, and lakes.

The Future

In the early 1990s, New Zealand began to recover from its most serious economic problems. Unemployment and inflation gradually declined, and cuts in government spending helped reduce public debt. With less government regulation of private companies, the country anticipates increased investment by domestic and foreign businesses. But some New Zealanders are still waiting for their standard of living to improve. Economic hardships remain for those who depend on government support, because many aid payments have been reduced to help the government achieve other economic goals.

Although New Zealand's continued economic growth depends on the expansion of nonagricultural industries, farming will remain the foundation of the economy. Fishing and forestry will continue to be important sources of income. As more tourists visit New Zealand, the country's economy may create more jobs and could

Courtesy of Ward Barrett

Wellington is situated in one of the most geologically unstable areas of New Zealand. These houses, as well as the main railways and highways into the city, are on the scarp (cliff) of a fault (fracture) along which an earthquake could occur. No part of New Zealand is completely free from the risk of earthquake damage.

The Maori called Mount Sefton *Maunga Atua*—"Mountain of the Gods"—because the peak seems to roar as avalanches send ice and rocks tumbling down its sides. Mount Sefton, in Mount Cook National Park, is one of 17 alps that tower above 10,000 feet. Protecting New Zealand's natural beauty for future generations is one of the country's national priorities.

be less dependent on world demand for agricultural products.

For several years, a lack of jobs increased tensions between the Maori and pakeha populations. The unemployment rate is much higher for the Maori than it is for pakehas, and wages and living standards are unequal between the two groups. A continuing challenge for New Zealand is to improve educational and work opportunities for the Maori and to work out fair settlements for longstanding grievances over land.

The country has also experienced tension in its relations with the United States.

The New Zealand government risked damaging its friendship with the United States to keep nuclear ships out of New Zealand's ports. Although the two countries no longer share military goals, their trading partnership and diplomatic relations are strong.

New Zealand is a country of great physical beauty. Its mountains, rivers, lakes, and coasts add to the quality of life its people share. Protecting the environment is important to New Zealanders. Preserving their natural resources while pursuing economic and social goals will be a continuing challenge in the coming years.

Index